Weekly Reader Books presents

Surviving Fights
with Your Brothers and Sisters

A Children's Book about Sibling Rivalry

by

Joy Wilt

Illustrated by Ernie Hergenroeder

Educational Products Division
Word, Incorporated
Waco, Texas

Author

JOY WILT is creator and director of Children's Ministries, an organization that provides resources "for people who care about children"—speakers, workshops, demonstrations, consulting services, and training institutes. A certified elementary school teacher, administrator, and early childhood specialist, Joy is also consultant to and professor in the master's degree program in children's ministries for Fuller Theological Seminary. Joy is a graduate of LaVerne College, LaVerne, California (B.A. in Biological Science), and Pacific Oaks College, Pasadena, California (M.A. in Human Development). She is author of three books, *Happily Ever After, An Uncomplicated Guide to Becoming a Superparent,* and *Taming the Big Bad Wolves,* as well as the popular *Can-Make-And-Do Books.* Joy's commitment "never to forget what it feels like to be a child" permeates the many innovative programs she has developed and her work as lecturer, consultant, writer, and—not least—mother of two children, Christopher and Lisa.

Artist

ERNIE HERGENROEDER is founder and owner of Hergie & Associates (a visual communications studio and advertising agency). With the establishment of this company in 1975, "Hergie" and his wife, Faith, settled in San Jose with their four children, Lynn, Kathy, Stephen, and Beth. Active in community and church affairs, Hergie is involved in presenting creative workshops for teachers, ministers, and others who wish to understand the techniques of communicating visually. He also lectures in high schools to encourage young artists toward a career in commercial art. Hergie serves as a consultant to organizations such as the Police Athletic League (PAL), Girl Scouts, and religious and secular corporations. His ultimate goal is to touch the hearts of kids (8 to 80) all over the world—visually!

This book is a presentation of Weekly Reader Books.
Weekly Reader Books offers book clubs for children from
preschool through junior high school.

For further information write to:
WEEKLY READER BOOKS
1250 Fairwood Ave.
Columbus, Ohio 43216

ISBN 0-8499-8125-5
Library of Congress Catalog Card Number: 78-66143

6 7 8 9 / 85 84 83 82

Contents

Introduction

Surviving Fights with Your Brothers and Sisters is one of a series of books. The complete set is called **Ready-Set-Grow!**

Surviving Fights with Your Brothers and Sisters deals with the friction that naturally exists between brothers and sisters. This book can be used by itself or as a part of a program that utilizes all of the **Ready-Set-Grow!** books.

Surviving Fights with Your Brothers and Sisters is specifically designed so that children can either read the book themselves or have it read to them. This can be done at home, church, or school. When reading to children, it is not necessary to complete the book at one sitting. Concern should be given to the attention span of the individual child and his or her comprehension of the subject matter.

Surviving Fights with Your Brothers and Sisters is designed to involve the child in the concepts that are being taught. This is done by simply and carefully explaining each concept and then asking questions that invite a response from the child. It is hoped that by answering the questions the child will personalize the concept and, thus, integrate it into his or her thinking.

Most brothers and sisters grow tired of being together. They get tired of eating, sleeping, playing, working, and going places together. Often children fight because they are simply tired of being with each other.

<u>Surviving Fights with Your Brothers and Sisters</u> offers definitions of and solutions to "sibling rivalry." A child begins to understand why he or she fights with his or her brothers and sisters. Examples and situations in this book ask the child:

Does it feel good to hurt each other's bodies?

Does it feel good to hurt each other's feelings?

Does it feel good to hurt each other's things?

<u>Surviving Fights with Your Brothers and Sisters</u> is designed to teach the child that brothers and sisters say and do mean things to each other, but that by learning to respect each other's bodies, thoughts, feelings, and desires they can learn to treat one another with kindness and love.

Surviving Fights with Your Brothers and Sisters

If you are someone's brother or sister . . .

this book is for you!

Have you ever had a brother or sister say
any of these things to you?

Have you ever said any of these things to a
brother or sister of yours?

If you have a brother or sister . . .

you have probably heard many of these things, and

you have probably said many of these things.

Every brother or sister has mean things said and done to him or her.

Every brother or sister says and does mean things.

13

There are a lot of reasons why brothers and sisters fight.

Chapter 1

Why Do Brothers and Sisters Fight?

REASON NUMBER ONE

Wishing Your Parents Loved You More than They Love Anyone Else

Most boys and girls love their parents more than anyone else in the world.

They love their parents:

more than they love their grandparents,

more than they love their aunts and uncles,

more than they love their friends, and

more than they love their brothers and sisters.

17

And so most boys and girls want their parents to love them more than anyone else in the world.

They want to be loved:

more than their grandparents are loved,

more than their aunts and uncles are loved,

more than their friends are loved, and

more than their brothers and sisters are loved.

19

Oftentimes a fight happens because a person wishes that his or her parents loved him or her more than another brother or sister.

21

Have you ever fought with your brother
or sister because you wished your parents
loved you more than the other brother or
sister?

If you have, you are like a lot of other
brothers and sisters in the world.

It may help to know that almost every
person in the world has wished that his
or her parents loved him or her more
than they love anyone else.

Because this is true . . .

you need to know and remember that even
though your parents try to love you and
your brothers and sisters fairly and equally,
they still love you in a very special way.
Why?

There is no one else in the whole world like
you.

You are one of a kind. No one can replace
you.

Because you are special, your parents love you in a very special way. They may not love you more than they love your brothers and sisters, but they love you in a way that is different from the way they love your brothers and sisters.

REASON NUMBER TWO

Wishing You Were the Best

Most boys and girls wish they were the best.
They wish they were . . .

the best in sports . . .

the best in school . . .

FINISH

REPORT CARD

And so most boys and girls do not like it when their brothers and sisters are better than they are.

They do not want their brothers and sisters to be:

better in sports,

better in school,

better looking, and

better at making things.

29

Oftentimes a fight happens because a person thinks that his or her brother or sister is better than he or she is.

31

Have you ever fought with your brother or sister because
you thought that he or she was better than you?

If you have, you are like a lot of other brothers and
sisters in the world.

It may help to know that almost every person in the world has wished that he or she was the best.

Because this is true . . .

you need to know and remember that no one person is best at everything.

Some people are the best at some things, while other people are the best at other things.

You are the best at some things, while your brothers and sisters are the best at other things. Your brothers and sisters may be better than you at some things, but that does not mean that they are better persons than you are.

35

REASON NUMBER THREE

Not Being Respected

Most boys and girls want to be respected. They want other people to respect their bodies . . .

respect their thoughts . . .

And so most boys and girls get upset when their bodies, their thoughts, their feelings, and their desires are not respected by their brothers and sisters.

Oftentimes a fight happens because a person does not feel respected by his or her brother or sister.

41

Have you ever fought with your brother
or sister because you thought that he
or she did not respect you?

If you have, you are like a lot of other
brothers and sisters in the world.

It may help to know that almost every person
in the world has a need to be respected.

Your brothers and sisters may not treat
you with respect, but that does not mean
that you are not a person worthy of respect.

45

REASON NUMBER FOUR

Being Treated Unfairly by Your Parents

Most boys and girls do not like to be treated unfairly by their parents. They feel that they are being treated unfairly when . . .

someone else receives more of something . . .

someone else receives more attention . . .

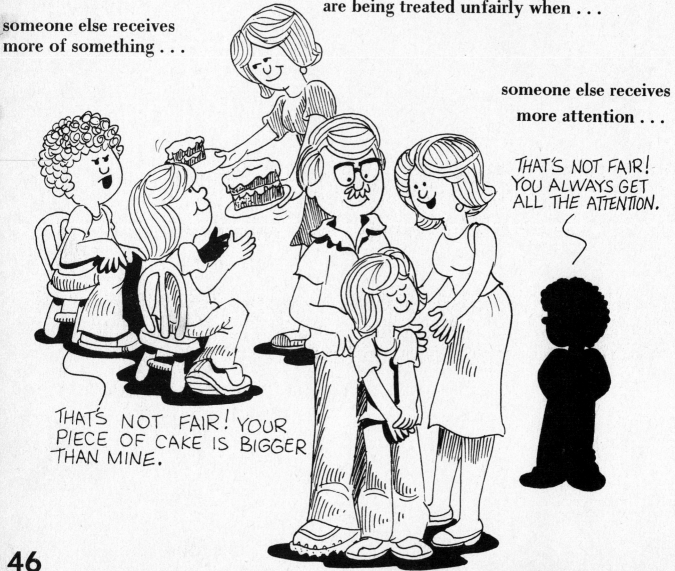

THAT'S NOT FAIR! YOU ALWAYS GET ALL THE ATTENTION.

THAT'S NOT FAIR! YOUR PIECE OF CAKE IS BIGGER THAN MINE.

someone else receives more privileges . . .

or someone else does not have to do as much work.

And so most boys and girls get angry when they are treated unfairly by their parents.

They feel that they are being treated unfairly when:

someone else receives more of something,

someone else receives more attention,

someone else receives more privileges, or

someone else does not have to do as much work.

Oftentimes a fight happens because a person feels his or her parents have treated him or her unfairly in favor of another brother or sister.

51

Have you ever fought with your brother or sister because you felt that you had been treated unfairly by your parents?

If you have, you are like a lot of other brothers and sisters in the world.

It may help to know that almost every person in the world does not like to be treated unfairly by his or her parents.

Because this is true . . .

you need to know and remember that you have a right to ask questions about the way you are being treated. If you ask your questions politely, you will usually receive honest answers.

Sometimes your questions will help your parents see that they are treating you unfairly and that they need to do something to correct the problem.

However . . .

Sometimes your questions will help you discover that you are not being treated unfairly. Asking questions should help you understand the situation better.

REASON NUMBER FIVE

Being Teased

Most boys and girls do not like
to be teased. They do not like to be
teased about how they look . . .

teased about what they think and feel . .

teased about what they do
and say . . .

And so most boys and girls get upset when they are teased by their brothers and sisters.

They get angry when they are teased about:

how they look,

what they think and feel,

what they say and do, or

what they like and don't like.

59

Oftentimes a fight happens
because a person is teased
by his or her brother or
sister.

Have you ever fought with your brother or sister because he or she teased you?

If you have, you are like a lot of other brothers and sisters in the world.

It may help to know that almost every person in the world does not like to be teased.

Because this is true . . .

you need to know and remember that you do not have to be teased. You do not have to stand and listen to someone tease you. You can walk away.

When your brother or sister starts to tease you, remember to walk away!

65

REASON NUMBER SIX
Being Embarrassed

HAVE YOU EVER NOTICED THE MOLES ON MY BROTHER'S FACE?

Most boys and girls do not want to be embarrassed by another person. They do not want to be embarrassed in front of adults . . .

embarrassed in front of teenagers . . .

DID YOU KNOW MY BROTHER STILL BELIEVES IN GHOSTS AND GOBLINS?

LIBRARY

embarrassed in front of other children . . .

or embarrassed in front of anyone.

And so most boys and girls get upset when they are embarrassed by their brothers and sisters.

They get angry when they are embarrassed:

in front of adults,

in front of teenagers,

in front of other children, or

in front of anyone.

Oftentimes a fight happens
because a person is embarrassed
by his or her brother or sister.

Have you ever fought with your brother or sister because he or she embarrassed you in front of another person?

If you have, you are like a lot of other brothers and sisters in the world.

It may help to know that almost every person in the world does not like to be embarrassed in front of other people.

Because this is true . . .

you need to know and remember that just as you do not like to be embarrassed, your brothers and sisters do not like to be embarrassed either.

The best thing for you to do is to make an agreement with your brothers and sisters.

Promise your brothers and sisters that you will never embarrass them if they will never embarrass you.

If your brothers and sisters should ever forget their promise and embarrass you, remember that you can always walk away. You don't have to stand there and be embarrassed.

I PROMISE THAT I WILL NEVER EMBARRASS YOU.
AND I PROMISE THAT I WILL NEVER EMBARRASS YOU.

REASON NUMBER SEVEN
Having Your Things Abused

Most boys and girls who own their own things want to keep them in good condition.

They do not want their things lost . . .

their things misused . . .

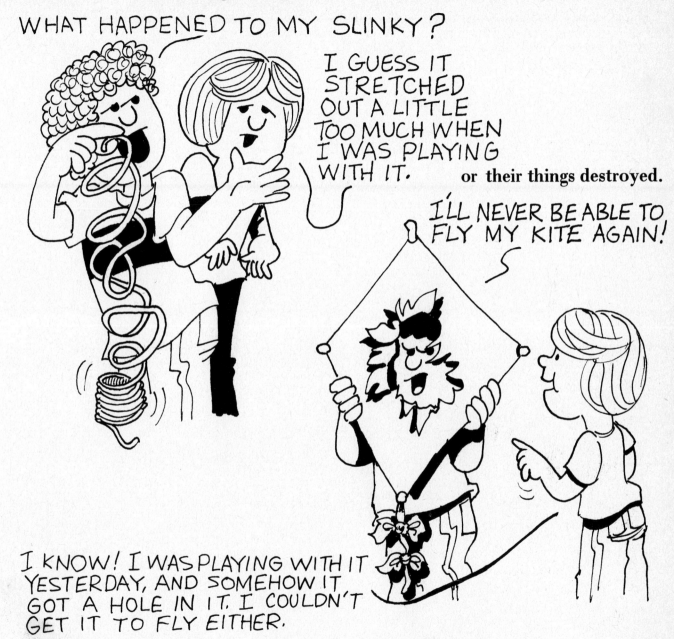

And so most boys and girls get upset when their things are abused by their brothers and sisters.

They get angry when their things are:

lost,

misused,

damaged, or

destroyed.

79

Oftentimes a fight happens because
a person has things that are lost,
misused, damaged, or destroyed
by his or her brother or sister.

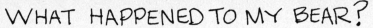

Have you ever fought with your brother or sister because he or she lost, misused, damaged, or destroyed your things?

If you have, you are like a lot of other brothers and sisters in the world.

It may help to know that almost every person in the world does not like to have his or her things lost, misused, damaged, or destroyed.

Because this is true . . .

you need to know and remember that the things that really belong to you are yours to keep. You have the responsibility to take care of those things.

Taking care of your things includes not loaning them to a brother or sister who will lose, misuse, damage, or destroy them.

This responsibility also includes putting your things away so that they will not be lost, misused, damaged, or destroyed by your brothers and sisters.

REASON NUMBER EIGHT
Being Together Too Much
Most boys and girls live together with their brothers and sisters.

They often . . .

eat together . . .

sleep together . . .

play and work together and . . .

go places together.

And so most boys and girls get tired of being together with their brothers and sisters.

They get tired of:

eating,

sleeping,

playing,

working, and

going places together.

89

Oftentimes a fight happens because
a person gets tired of being together
with his or her brother or sister.

Have you ever fought with your brother or sister because you got tired of being together with him or her?

If you have, you are like a lot of other brothers and sisters in the world.

It may help to know that almost every person in the world would get tired of another person if they had to be together too much.

Because this is true . . .

you need to know and remember that sometimes you should get away from your brothers and sisters. This is so you won't get tired of them and start fighting.

Can you think of ways you can get away from your brothers and sisters?

94

95

Think about it.

Why do you fight with your brothers and sisters?

Do you fight with your brothers and sisters because:

you wish your parents loved you more than they love them,

you wish you were better than your brothers and sisters,

you are not being respected by them,

you are being treated unfairly by your parents,

you are being teased by your brothers and sisters,

you are being embarrassed by them,

you are having your things abused by them, or

you are being together with them too much?

Think about it some more.

Why do your brothers and sisters fight with you?

Do your brothers and sisters fight with you because:

they wish your parents loved them more than they love you,

they wish they were better than you,

they are not being respected by you,

they are being treated unfairly by your parents,

they are being teased by you,

they are being embarrassed by you,

they are having their things abused by you, or

they are being together with you too much?

A lot of things happen when you

fight with your brothers and

sisters . . .

Chapter 2

What Happens When You Fight with Your Brothers and Sisters?

There are a lot of things that might happen when you fight with a brother or sister. You may end up . . .

Hurting Each Other's Body

When you fight with your brother or sister, do you hurt each other's body?

Hurting Each Other's Feelings

When you fight with your brother or sister, do
you hurt each other's feelings?

Hurting Each Other's Things

When you fight with your brother or sister, do you hurt each other's things?

106

After you have hurt:

each other's body,

each other's feelings, or

each other's things,

what do you think?

Does it do any good to hurt:

each other's body,

each other's feelings, or

each other's things?

Does it help anybody in any way?

Probably not!

It is good to know why a fight starts.

It is good to know what happens during a fight.

It is even better to know that . . .

There are several good ways to handle fights with your brothers and sisters.

Chapter 3

How to Handle Fights with Your Brothers and Sisters

Step Number One

Think before You Fight

Remember:

Your parents love you in a very special way.

Your brothers and sisters are not better persons than you are.

You were created to be a person worthy of respect.

You should ask questions whenever you think you are being treated unfairly.

Walk away if you are being teased.

Make an agreement with your brothers and sisters
that you will not embarrass one another.

Put your things away so that they will not be
abused, and do not loan them to any brother
or sister who will not take care of them.

Spend some time away from your brothers and
sisters so that you won't get tired of being together.

Step Number Two
<u>Talk about It</u>

When your brother or sister wants to start a fight with you, stand face to face with him or her, look straight in his or her eyes, ask why he or she wants to fight with you . . .

tell how you feel and what you think and . . .

ask him or her not to fight with you. If he or she still wants to fight and won't talk to you . . .

Step Number Three

<u>Walk or Run Away</u>

If he or she still wants to fight and comes after you . . .

Step Number Four

Go Get Help

Go get help from an older person like a parent,
a teacher, or perhaps a baby sitter.

Ask any of these persons to help you settle the fight.

123

Remember:

Almost every person in the whole world has,
at one time or another, wished that he or
she didn't have any brothers or sisters.

Maybe at times you wish you didn't have any brothers or sisters.

But before you wish too hard, remember . . .

Life would be pretty boring and . . .

things would be awfully lonely . . .

Without brothers and sisters.